## DATE DUE

| | | |
|---|---|---|
| DE 20'06 | FEB 06 2016 | |
| FE 07'07 | | |
| | | |
| AP 13'07 | WITHDRAWN | |
| JY 30'07 | | |
| SE 29'07 | | |
| MY 16'08 | | |
| OR 26'09 | | |
| FEB 12 2015 | | |
| | | |
| | | |
| | | |
| | | |
| | | |
| | | |

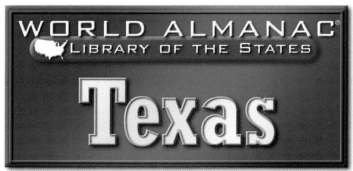

## THE LONE STAR STATE

*by Rachel Barenblat*

Curriculum Consultant: Jean Craven,
Director of Instructional Support,
Albuquerque, NM, Public Schools

**WORLD ALMANAC® LIBRARY**

Please visit our web site at: **www.worldalmanaclibrary.com**
For a free color catalog describing World Almanac® Library's list of high-quality books and multimedia programs, call 1-800-848-2928 (USA) or 1-800-387-3178 (Canada). World Almanac® Library's fax: (414) 332-3567.

**Library of Congress Cataloging-in-Publication Data**

Barenblat, Rachel.
    Texas, the Lone Star State / by Rachel Barenblat.
        p. cm. — (World Almanac Library of the states)
    Includes bibliographical references and index.
    Summary: Illustrations and text present the history, geography, people, politics and government, economy, and social life and customs of Texas, whose motto is "Friendship."
    ISBN 0-8368-5121-8 (lib. bdg.)
    ISBN 0-8368-5292-3 (softcover)
    1. Texas—Juvenile literature. [1. Texas.] I. Title. II. Series.
    F386.3.B37   2002
    976.4—dc21                                                                2001046984

This edition first published in 2002 by
**World Almanac® Library**
330 West Olive Street, Suite 100
Milwaukee, WI  53212  USA

Design and Editorial: **Jack&Bill**/Bill SMITH STUDIO Inc.
Editors: Jackie Ball and Kristen Behrens
Art Directors: Ron Leighton and Jeffrey Rutzky
Photo Research and Buying: Christie Silver and Sean Livingstone
Design and Production: Maureen O'Connor and Jeffrey Rutzky
World Almanac® Library Editors: Patricia Lantier, Amy Stone, Valerie J. Weber, Catherine Gardner, Carolyn Kott Washburne, Alan Wachtel, Monica Rausch
World Almanac® Library Production: Scott M. Krall and Eva Erato-Rudek, Tammy Gruenewald, Katherine A. Goedheer

Photo credits: p. 4–5 © PhotoDisc; p. 6 (top) © Corel, (bottom) © PhotoDisc; p. 7 (top) National Cowboy and Western Heritage Museum, (bottom) Dr. Pepper Museum; p. 9 © Corel; p. 10 © PhotoDisc; p. 11 © Carl Mydans/TimePix; p. 12 © PhotoDisc; p. 13 © Library of Congress; p. 14 (all) © Library of Congress; p. 15 courtesy of the Kerrville CVB; p. 17 © Carrol Barrington; p. 18 © PhotoDisc; p. 19 courtesy of the Waco CVB; p. 20 (from left to right) courtesy of Galveston CVB, © Richard Reynolds, © Carrol Barrington, p. 21 (all) © Corel; p. 23 © Corel; p. 26 (all) © PhotoDisc; p. 27 © Corel; p. 29 (top) © Library of Congress, (bottom) © J. Griffis Smith; p. 30 © Bettmann/CORBIS; p. 31 (all) © Library of Congress; p. 32 (top) © PhotoDisc (bottom) © Library of Congress; p. 33 © Neal Preston/CORBIS; p. 34 (all) courtesy of Austin CVB, p. 35 courtesy of Amarillo CVC; p. 36 S. A. Convention and Visitors Bureau/Al Rendon; p. 37 courtesy of Amarillo CVC; p. 39 (left) © Artville, (top right) © Time Magazine/Time Inc., (bottom right) © Artville; p. 40 (from left to right) © PhotoDisc, © Sahm Doherty/TimePix; p. 41 (from left to right) © Artville, p. 42–43 © Library of Congress; p. 44 © Scott Newton/Austin City Limits; p. 45 (top) courtesy of Galveston CVB, (bottom) courtesy of SACVB/Morris Goen

Printed in the United States of America

2 3 4 5 6 7 8 9 07 06 05 04 03

# Texas

# Big Is Only the Beginning

Ask anyone for one word to describe Texas and what you would hear, overwhelmingly, would be "big." There's no doubt about it: The Lone Star State IS big. Huge, in fact. Alaska is the only state bigger. Texas sits at the bottom center of the contiguous (touching) states like a giant, saddle-shaped building block, forming a massive foundation solid enough to support all the states above.

If Texas were a sheet of rolled-out dough, there would be enough to cut out about 250 Rhode Island-sized cookies. That's nothing though. Texas is as big or bigger than many countries in the world. For example, Italy and Japan combined could both fit inside Texas's borders.

Big, however, is only the beginning of what Texas is all about. Inside its borders are scenes of spectacular natural beauty in an astonishing variety of environments: prairie, grassland, desert, forest, and coast. Its richness extends to other natural resources, such as oil and natural gas, which made Texas, in the twentieth century, the energy capital of the United States.

When it comes to Texans, they have a reputation for being as big as their state — if not necessarily in size, in the bigger-than-life tradition that springs from the state's famous and ferocious fighting spirit. Who could forget Alamo heroes Davy Crockett and Jim Bowie? That stubborn, single-minded quest for independence helped Texans "Remember the Alamo" and win the war to end Mexican rule. Beginning with the first visit by European explorers in 1519, six different flags have flown over Texas. They are the flags of Spain, France, Mexico, the Republic of Texas, the Confederacy, and the United States. Texas has long been a frontier state, attracting explorers and settlers. Its borders have been the scenes of fierce battles for conquest and for independence.

The fighting spirit may no longer be about defending borders, but it's still there. Texas will always continue to fight to live life as it pleases, whatever the consequences.

▶ Map of Texas, showing interstate highway system, as well as major cities.

▼ A rocket at the National Aeronautics and Space Administration (NASA) center in Houston.

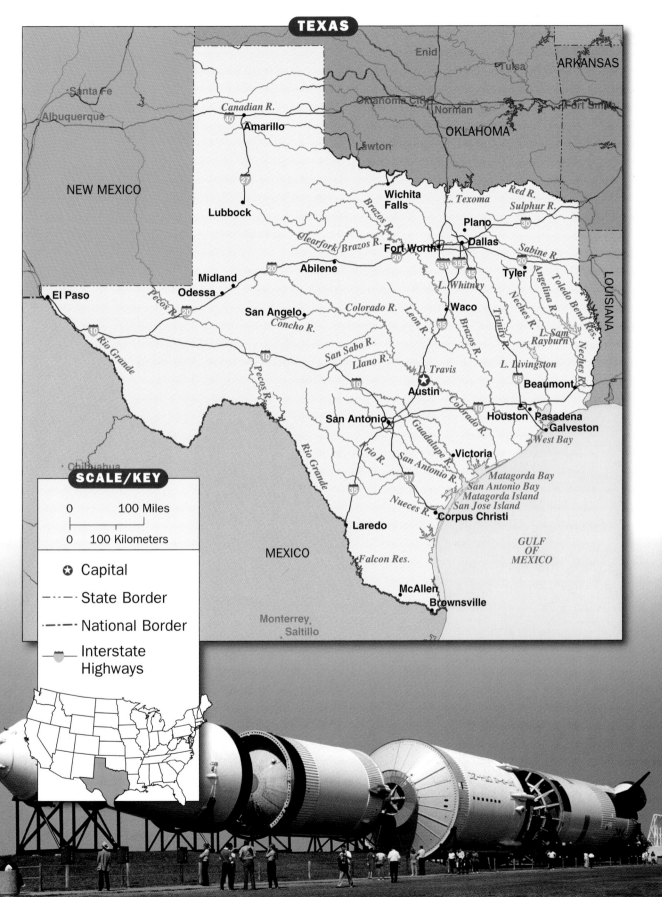

# TEXAS

ARKANSAS

Enid

Tulsa

Fort Smith

Santa Fe

Albuquerque

Oklahoma City

Norman

OKLAHOMA

NEW MEXICO

Canadian R.

**Amarillo**

Lawton

Lubbock

Wichita Falls

L. Texoma

Red R.

Sulphur R.

Brazos R.

Clearfork

Brazos R.

**Plano**

**Dallas**

Sabine R.

**Fort Worth**

**Tyler**

Angelina R.

Toledo Bend Res.

LOUISIANA

Midland

**Abilene**

L. Whitney

Neches R.

Odessa

El Paso

Pecos R.

Colorado R.

**Waco**

L. Sam Rayburn

Neches R.

San Angelo

Concho R.

Leon R.

Brazos R.

Trinity R.

Rio Grande

San Sabo R.

L. Livingston

**Beaumont**

Llano R.

L. Travis

**Austin**

Colorado R.

**Houston** **Pasadena**

**Galveston**

Pecos R.

**San Antonio**

Guadalupe R.

West Bay

**Victoria**

Chihuahua

Frio R.

San Antonio R.

Matagorda Bay

San Antonio Bay

Matagorda Island

San Jose Island

Nueces R.

**Corpus Christi**

Rio Grande

**Laredo**

MEXICO

Falcon Res.

GULF OF MEXICO

Monterrey

Saltillo

McAllen

**Brownsville**

## SCALE/KEY

0 — 100 Miles

0 — 100 Kilometers

✪ Capital

-··-··- State Border

-·-·- National Border

Interstate Highways

# Fast Facts

## Texas (TX), The Lone Star State

### Entered Union

Entered Union: December 29, 1845 (28th state)

| Capital | Population |
| --- | --- |
| Austin | 656,562 |

### Total Population (2000)

20,851,820 (2nd most populous state)

| Largest Cities | Population |
| --- | --- |
| Houston | 1,953,631 |
| Dallas | 1,188,580 |
| San Antonio | 1,144,646 |
| Austin | 656,562 |
| El Paso | 563,662 |

### Land Area

261,797 square miles (678,054 square kilometers) (2nd largest state)

### State Motto

Friendship — *The state's name, Texas, may derive from the word that means "friend" in the Caddo language. The Caddo were one of the Native American groups that lived in Texas.*

### State Song

"Texas, Our Texas" — *lyrics by William J. Marsh and Gladys Y. Wright, music by William J. Marsh.*

### State Mammal (large)

Longhorn Cattle

### State Mammal (small)

Armadillo

### State Mammal (flying)

Mexican Free-tailed Bat

### State Bird

Mockingbird — *On average, the mockingbird has twenty-five to thirty songs in its repertoire.*

### State Fish

Guadalupe Bass

### State Insect

Monarch Butterfly — *This butterfly does not hibernate but migrates over the course of the changing seasons.*

### State Tree

Pecan — *The only nut tree native to North America. Texas is the largest producer of native pecan nuts and is second only to Georgia in the production of hybrid pecan nuts.*

### State Flower

Bluebonnet — *This flower is also known as buffalo clover, wolf flower, and* el conejo.

### State Plant

Prickly Pear Cactus

### State Pepper

Jalapeño

### State Fruit

Texas Red Grapefruit

### State Gem

Blue Topaz

### State Sport

Rodeo

## PLACES TO VISIT

**Big Bend National Park,** *near Sturdy Butte*
Big Bend was the first national park in Texas. Its 1,250 square miles (3,238 square km) include the Rio Grande, canyons, plains, and the Chisos Mountains. The park also features forests of petrified wood from millions of years ago. More than half the species of birds found in North America are found in Big Bend National Park.

**The Alamo,** *San Antonio*
The Alamo is known as "the cradle of Texas liberty." Originally a church named San Antonio de Valero, it was abandoned in 1793. It was used as a fortress during the Texas Revolution. One of the most famous battles of the revolution was fought there. The name *Alamo* comes from a grove of cottonwoods (*álamos* in Spanish) that grew nearby when the mission was built.

**For other places and events to attend, see p. 44**

## BIGGEST, BEST, AND MOST

- Greatest variety of flowers
- Greatest variety of reptiles
- Only state with five major ports

## STATE FIRSTS

- The oldest cave paintings in the United States were discovered in caves near the Pecos River. The paintings were made nearly four thousand years ago.
- The first permanent European settlement in what is now Texas was Ysleta, founded in 1682.
- In 1925 Miriam Ferguson was the first woman in the United States elected governor, in Texas.
- The first nonstop round-the-world airplane flight left from Fort Worth on February 26, 1949, and returned on March 2, ninety-four hours and one minute later.

## Ride 'Em Cowboy!

In the years following the Civil War, many former slaves became cowboys. African-American cowboys were found in great numbers on the Coastal Plain between the Sabine and Guadalupe Rivers. Others became rodeo riders and federal peace officers. Among the most famous was William Pickett, a rodeo star. He is credited with inventing the rodeo sport known as "bulldogging" and was inducted into the Cowboy Hall of Fame in 1971.

## Birthplace of a Soft Drink

Morrison's Old Corner Drug Store in Waco, Texas, was the birthplace of Dr. Pepper soda in 1885. Charles Alderton, a pharmacist at the drug store, is credited with creating this carbonated drink. Dr. Pepper is the oldest major soft drink available in the United States today. Alderton named it after Dr. Kenneth Pepper, his former boss back in Virginia. Virginians claim that Alderton, who eloped with Dr. Pepper's daughter, stole the formula.

# Lone Star Struggles and Strides

> It is impossible to exaggerate the pleasant character, the beauty, and the fertility of the province of Tejas . . .
> — *Father Antonio Olivares, 1716*

The earliest inhabitants of Texas were indigenous peoples who settled the region thousands of years ago. Most of these tribes were nomadic; they hunted with flint-tipped spears. In East Texas, which received more rain and was more fertile than the rest of the state, tribes settled in villages.

At the time when the first Europeans entered Texas, several tribes of Native Americans were inhabitants of the land. Among them were the Karankawa, nomads of the southern Gulf Coast; the Apache, who hunted buffalo on the high plains; and the Caddo, who lived in villages in the eastern pine forests.

The Karankawa were hunters and gathered wild plants. Little is known about their organization except that they had war leaders and hereditary chiefs.

Several different Apache tribes lived in the American West when Europeans first entered Texas. Although the tribes differed, all were hunter-gatherers. They tracked buffalo, gathered wild plants, farmed, and occasionally raided other tribes or villages. Although they were initially friendly toward Europeans and U.S. settlers, relations broke down in the early seventeenth century.

The Caddo were a group of several tribes who shared a common language. They lived in cone-shaped dwellings covered with grass and grouped around temple mounds. The Caddo were potters and basket makers and wove cloth from grasses.

Both French and Spanish explorers wanted Caddo territory, and by the late 1700s the Caddo tribes were broken up. In 1855 Caddo in neighboring regions were

| Native American Groups in Texas |
|---|
| Apache |
| Caddo |
| Coahuiltecan |
| Commanche |
| Karankawa |
| Lipan, or Lipan-Apache |
| Tonkawa |
| Other related Apache groups, especially the Mescalero-Apache |

forced to relocate to Texas. The Caddo in Texas then fled to Oklahoma in 1859 because of threats of massacre and were given a reservation there on the Washita River.

## Age of Exploration

In 1519 the Spanish explorer Alonso Alvarez de Pineda was looking for riches to bring back to Spain. He was the first European to visit Texas and made the first map of the Gulf Coast. In 1528 Pánfilo de Narváez, a Spanish explorer, came to Texas. He and his men were shipwrecked near what is now Galveston. Of the nearly 250 men in the expedition, only 4 survived. Álvar Núñez Jérez de la Frontera Cabeza de Vaca, the treasurer of Narváez's expedition, later became an explorer himself. In 1682, the Spanish established Corpus Christi de la Isleta, their first mission in Texas.

**DID YOU KNOW?**

Six different flags have flown over Texas during eight changes of sovereignty. Spain claimed the land first in 1519. France gained a claim to the area in the 1680s, when Robert Cavelier, sieur de La Salle, established Fort St. Louis. In 1690, Spain reclaimed Texas, but Mexico overthrew the Spanish government and established an independent nation in 1821. Later, Texans won their independence from Mexico and formed the Republic of Texas in 1836. Texas joined the United States in 1845, joined the Confederate States of America in 1861, and was readmitted to the United States in 1870.

## Mexican Texas and the Texan Revolution

*I shall never surrender or retreat.*
— William Barrett Travis, the Alamo, 1836

Mexicans overthrew the Spanish government in 1821. In the same year, an Anglo-American named Stephen F. Austin gained permission from Mexico to bring Anglo settlers into Mexican territory. They settled in several colonies along the Colorado and Brazos Rivers.

In 1833 Mexican General Santa Anna staged a coup and took over Mexico. Most Texans initially supported Santa Anna, but the Texans wanted greater self-government, and Santa Anna would not allow it. Mexico also tried to outlaw slavery, but many white settlers relied on slave labor. In the period between 1821 and 1836, as many as five thousand Africans and African Americans were brought to the region as slaves. By 1835 tensions were running high between the Mexican government and the Texans. Many Texans wanted to arm themselves and fight for independence. On October 2 a group of Mexican troops tried to take a cannon from the Texans in the town of Gonzales. The Texans, waving a flag

▲ Mission San José y San Miguel de Aguayo was one of a chain of five missions established along the San Antonio River in the 1700s.

that said "Come and Take It," fired on the Mexicans and drove them away. Riders on horseback distributed signs that said: "Freemen of Texas — To Arms!!! To Arms!!! — Now's the day, and now's the hour!" The Texas Revolution had begun.

In 1836 the Texans issued a declaration of independence at a place they called Washington-on-the-Brazos. A string of battles followed as the Texans fought for independence from Mexico. The best known of these battles is the siege of a small fortress in San Antonio known as the Alamo. The siege lasted from February 23 to March 6, 1836.

General Santa Anna led about four thousand troops north to stop the uprising as a small band of Texas rebels holed up in the Alamo, determined not to surrender. They knew they were not likely to defeat the Mexican army, but wanted to hold back Mexican forces long enough for a larger Texas army to form.

For twelve days and nights, the Mexican forces bombarded the Alamo. On March 6 the Mexicans poured over the walls and took the fortress. About 189 Texans were killed, as were about 600 Mexicans. Frontiersmen Davy Crockett and Jim Bowie were among the Anglos killed in the battle of the Alamo. Jim Bowie is remembered today for the special knife he carried, which we now call a "bowie knife." About fifteen women and children found hiding in the chapel were spared. Three weeks later Santa Anna's troops captured nearly four hundred Texan soldiers near Goliad and executed all of them. These two bloody battles led to the war cry, "Remember the Alamo! Remember Goliad!"

General Sam Houston was commander in chief of the Texan forces in 1836. After the Alamo fell, he gathered about nine hundred men to fight for Texas. They retreated to a wooded spot on the San Jacinto River and waited. Santa Anna's army arrived on April 21 and set up camp. All through the night the Mexicans

# Texas Rangers

**B**ecause early colonists were often attacked by robbers, bandits, and hostile bands of Native Americans, Stephen F. Austin created "ranging companies" to guard the settlers. The first company, organized in 1823, consisted of only ten men. The rangers were the only lawmen in Texas for many years and earned the reputation of being tough and effective. To become a Ranger, it was said that a man had to "ride like a Mexican, track like a Comanche, shoot like a Kentuckian, and fight like the devil." In 1835 the rangers were officially organized into the Texas Rangers; they still exist today and are called in to help police and sheriffs with difficult situations. They wear no official uniform other than a white cowboy hat. Today there are more than one hundred Texas Rangers, both men and women.

prepared for a dawn attack that did not come. By afternoon Santa Anna allowed his men to sleep.

At 4:30 P.M., the Texans stormed the camp, shouting "Remember the Alamo! Remember Goliad!" The battle lasted only twenty minutes, but the killing went on for hours, as many Texan soldiers sought revenge for their comrades. General Houston rode among his troops and tried to stop the killing. General Santa Anna, found hiding in a marsh wearing a private's uniform, was captured. Texas had won its freedom from Mexican rule.

The Texas Revolution was not a simple fight between Anglos and Mexicans. Mexicans fought on both sides, and many were leaders of the revolution.

After the revolution Texas became a republic. Times were difficult and money was in short supply. Plus, Native tribes and bands of Mexicans periodically raided Texas towns around the border. Men called "rangers," who protected the settlers before the revolution, officially formed the Texas Rangers, a special police force.

Many Texans wanted to join the United States, and Texas was annexed by the United States in 1845, becoming the Union's twenty-eighth state.

▼ Like Mission San José *(see p. 10),* the Alamo was built to expand Spain's influence northward from Mexico. Instead it became a legend as the last stand of Texans fighting for independence. Today the mission, in San Antonio, is a national historic site.

## Boundary Disputes and Wars

*I protest against surrendering the Federal Constitution
. . . and to accept in its stead a so-called Confederate
Government . . .*
— Sam Houston, 1861

In the middle of the nineteenth century, the United
States and Mexico went to war in what is known as the
Mexican-American war, or *La Guerra de Estados Unidos
a Mexico* (War of the United States Against Mexico). Mexico
opposed Texas becoming part of the United States and was
also involved in a border dispute with Texas, which became
the cause of the war: Mexico believed that the southernmost border of Texas should be the Nueces River; the
United States wanted the border between Mexico and
Texas to be the Rio Grande.

On February 2, 1848, the United States and Mexico
ended the war with the Treaty of Guadalupe Hidalgo. The
treaty drew the boundary between the United States and
Mexico at the Rio Grande and Gila River. It also
established that, for $15 million, the United States would
receive more than 525,000 square miles (1,359,750 sq km)
of land (now Arizona, California, western Colorado,
Nevada, New Mexico, Texas, and Utah) from Mexico.

In the United States, the acquisition of all this territory
reopened the question of slavery's expansion.

Throughout the first half of the 1800s, Congress debated
whether or not to admit into the Union new states that
allowed slavery. While Texas had entered the Union as a
"slave" state, arguments raged over the question of slavery
in the territory gained in the Mexican-American War.

A desire on the part of Texas plantation owners to
maintain slavery was one of the reasons Texas joined the
Confederacy during the Civil War. At that point, there were
182,000 slaves in Texas — 30 percent of the population. As
in most of the Southern states that opposed abolition, the
people who had the most money and political power also
tended to be slave owners.

Not all slave owners, however, wanted Texas to secede
from the Union. Sam Houston, who became governor in
1859, opposed secession. After the state seceded in 1861, he
was turned out of office.

Texas was readmitted to the United States on March 30,
1870, five years after the Civil War was over.

### Spindletop

**O**n January 10, 1901, an
enormous explosion was
heard as a huge column
of oil poured from the
ground under a drilling
rig on Spindletop Hill,
near Beaumont. First,
mud bubbled; then six
tons of drilling pipe flew
out of the ground.
Startled roughnecks, or
oil workers, fled as the
pipe was followed by
mud, then gas, then oil.
The well was capped
nine days later; during
those nine days, nine
hundred thousand
barrels of oil poured out
of the ground! Its
discovery marked the
start of the modern oil
and gas industry. After
Spindletop, people spent
billions of dollars looking
for oil in Texas; the
cheap fuel they found
helped revolutionize
American transportation.

◀ The life experiences of former slaves were preserved by the Works Project Administration (WPA), a federal agency that conducted interviews during the 1930s. At left, Green Cumby, age eighty-six, sits outside his home in Abilene, Texas, in June 1937, after having told of his life in slavery in Texas. *Inset:* The WPA worker's transcript of the interview.

## The Cowboy Era

When slavery was abolished, many of the large cotton plantations that relied on forced labor could no longer operate. Cotton production declined, but a new industry flourished — cattle ranching.

In the early 1800s the first cowboys were Spanish *vaqueros*. They used lariats (lassos) and spurs, rode in saddles designed for cattle herding, and branded cattle to make it easier to identify which cows belonged to whom. After the Civil War cattle ranching became a big industry in Texas, staffed by U.S. cowboys who learned these skills from their Spanish counterparts.

Between eight and twelve cowboys handled each herd (roughly twenty-five hundred animals). Every fall they rounded up the cattle and branded them with the rancher's insignia or initials; every spring they drove the cattle to the railroad to sell them. Sometimes it was hundreds of miles to the nearest railroad.

From 1867 to 1887 more than six million longhorn cattle were moved from the Texas prairie to stockyards in Kansas and Missouri. By 1890 most cowboys marked ranches with barbed-wire boundaries, usually near railroads. When railroads became commonplace in Texas, the great trail drives stopped.

Railroads linked Texas with the world. Manufacturing, which had become an important element of the Texas economy during the Civil War, continued to grow as a result of the railroads. In 1901 Spindletop — the state's first oil gusher — was discovered near Beaumont, in East Texas. It signaled the beginning of the state's oil boom.

▲ A longhorn steer. The distance between the tips of the horns can be as much as 8 feet (2.4 meters).

## The Twentieth Century

*All I have I would have given gladly not to be standing here today.*
— Lyndon B. Johnson, assuming the presidency after the assassination of John F. Kennedy, 1963

At the dawn of the twentieth century, Texas's population had grown to more than three million. During the first half of the century, World War I, the Great Depression, and World War II affected Texas as well as the rest of the country. Texan soldiers fought in both world wars, and most Texans had a very hard time during the Depression, when jobs were scarce.

In 1925 Miriam A. Ferguson became the second woman to serve as a governor in the United States and the first elected in her own right. She served from 1925 to 1927 and again from 1933 to 1935. In her first term she battled Prohibition and the Ku Klux Klan. In her second term she tried to ease the hardships of the Great Depression. She ran unsuccessfully for governor a third time in 1940.

Dallas was the scene of the assassination, on November 22, 1963, of President John F. Kennedy. Vice President Lyndon Johnson of Texas, long a powerful figure in state and national politcs, was sworn in as president.

Today Texas is like a patchwork quilt. Cowboys still exist, although now they use jeeps or helicopters to round up animals. Oil is still important, although new gushers like Spindletop don't happen often anymore. Texas is still a frontier state, but today the pioneers are conquering space, the final frontier, from the National Aeronautics and Space Administration (NASA) space center in Houston.

**DID YOU KNOW?**

**A**lthough African Americans prospered in Texas during the period of Reconstruction after the Civil War, harsh laws instituted in 1902 took away most of their gains. In the 1890s more than one hundred thousand African Americans voted in state elections. In 1906 fewer than five thousand voted. The African-American population in Texas began to fall from 20 percent at the beginning of the twentieth century to about 12 percent today.

# High Times in Texas

> Texas is a state of mind. Texas is an obsession.
> Above all, Texas is a nation in every sense of the word . . . .
> A Texan outside of Texas is a foreigner.
>
> — *John Steinbeck,* Travels with Charley:
> In Search of America, *1962*

Today there are over twenty million Texans. Like most states, Texas has a diverse population. Although there is significant immigration, the majority of the state's current inhabitants were born there. Many Texans are descended from the state's original Native American inhabitants or from early Hispanic or Latino settlers; others stem from Stephen F. Austin's early Anglo settlers.

## Getting to Texas

Many people emigrated to Texas once it became a state. The port of Galveston is sometimes called the "Ellis Island of Texas," after the island in New York that, in the nineteenth and twentieth centuries, served as the port of entry for many new Americans. Between 1840 and 1860

| Age Distribution of Texans (approximate) | |
|---|---|
| 0–4 | 1,624,628 |
| 5–19 | 4,921,608 |
| 20–24 | 1,539,404 |
| 25–44 | 6,484,321 |
| 45–64 | 3,507,658 |
| 65 & over | 2,072,532 |

## Across One Hundred Years

### Texas's three largest foreign-born groups for 1890 and 1990

**1890**

| Mexico | Germany | England |
|---|---|---|
| 51,559 | 48,843 | 9,441 |

Total state population: 2,235,527
Total foreign-born: 152,956 (7%)

**1990**

| Mexico | Vietnam | El Salvador |
|---|---|---|
| 907,432 | 53,628 | 49,419 |

Total state population: 16,986,510
Total foreign-born: 1,524,436 (9%)

## Patterns of Immigration

The total number of people who immigrated to Texas in 1998 was 44,248. Of that number, the largest immigrant groups were from Mexico (51%), India (6%), and Vietnam (2%).

more than a quarter of a million people passed through Galveston. Some had arrived directly from Europe, while others entered the United States first through another port and then traveled on to Texas.

Many colonists came to Texas from Germany, Britain, Ireland, France, Czechoslovakia, and other European countries. Europeans tended to settle together in small communities where they could speak their native languages and eat familiar foods. Many small towns like Fredericksburg and Castroville still maintain vestiges of these cultures in their food and architecture.

In the late nineteenth century, the first Chinese immigrants came to Texas to work on the railroads. Today the state is home to many Asian-American Texans. By far,

## Heritage and Background, Texas — Year 2000

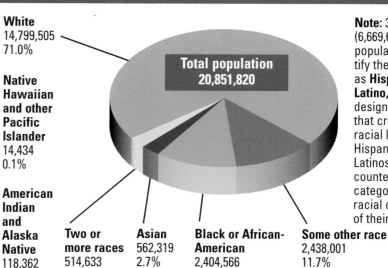

▶ Here is a look at the racial backgrounds of Texans today. Texas ranks eighteenth among all U.S. states with regard to African Americans as a percentage of the population, although in sheer numbers it has the third-largest African-American population.

**White**
14,799,505
71.0%

**Native Hawaiian and other Pacific Islander**
14,434
0.1%

**American Indian and Alaska Native**
118,362
0.6%

**Two or more races**
514,633
2.5%

**Asian**
562,319
2.7%

**Black or African-American**
2,404,566
11.5%

**Some other race**
2,438,001
11.7%

Total population
20,851,820

**Note:** 32% (6,669,666) of the population identify themselves as **Hispanic** or **Latino,** a cultural designation that crosses racial lines. Hispanics and Latinos are counted in this category and the racial category of their choice.

however, the largest minority in Texas is the Latino population. Latinos, people of Latin-American or Mexican descent living in the United States, make up 32 percent of the people living in Texas today. In some cities, such as San Antonio, more than half the population is Latino.

Texas is also part-time home to many Mexican migrant workers, many of whom cross the border illegally because they can make better wages in the United States than they can in Mexico. Life is difficult and often unsafe for illegal immigrants in Texas and throughout the United States.

Texas remains one of the fastest-growing states in the country. Between 1970 and 1990 its population growth rate was about two-and-a-half times the national average. From 1990 to 2000 the growth rate was almost 23%, nearly twice

| Educational Levels of Texas Workers | |
| --- | --- |
| Less than 9th grade | 1,382,528 |
| 9th to 12th grade, no diploma | 1,485,031 |
| High school graduate, including equivalency | 2,640,162 |
| Some college, no degree | 2,171,439 |
| Associate degree | 531,540 |
| Bachelor's degree | 1,428,031 |
| Graduate or professional degree | 666,874 |

▼ The Dallas skyline.

the national average, as Texas gained close to four million new residents. The many cultures of Texas are celebrated each August in the Texas Folklife Festival in San Antonio. Visitors to the festival can sample the food, music, and dance of the many ethnic groups that have made Texas their home.

Texans today come from almost every racial and cultural background imaginable. The top three ancestries in Texas are Mexican, German, and Irish. Twenty percent of Texans claim Mexican ancestry; 17 percent are of German descent, and 13 percent have Irish ancestry.

▲ A Latino celebration at St. Francis on the Brazos in Waco.

## Education

About 30 percent of the total population over the age of three is enrolled in school, making Texas sixth in the nation in school enrollment. Thirteen percent of the population over 25 have only finished school through the eighth grade; 72 percent of those over 25 have finished high school; 20 percent of those over 25 have attained (or are in the process of attaining) college degrees.

## Religion

There is religious diversity in Texas, although most of it is within the various denominations of Christianity. Texan Christians include Catholics, Baptists, Methodists, and members of many other denominations. Overall, about 90 percent of Texans are Christians, 0.7 percent are Jewish, 0.2 percent are Muslim, 0.2 percent are Buddhist, 0.2 percent are Unitarian, 0.6 percent are agnostic (people who neither believe nor disbelieve in God), and 4.9 percent of Texans say they belong to no religion at all.

## A Cultural Blend

Because Texas was once part of Mexico, and still shares a large border with that country, its culture has been strongly influenced by Mexican culture. Mexican food, music, and art are popular throughout Texas. In some areas, distinctions between the two cultures have blurred, giving birth to Tex-Mex cuisine and *Tejano,* a musical blend that draws from instruments and styles on both sides of the border.

Mexico is not the only nation to have an impact on Texan culture; many other peoples have settled in Texas, too. Today the state continues to grow, becoming ever more diverse.

# A State of Amazement

> I must say as to what I have seen of Texas, it is the garden spot of the world, the best land and the best prospects for health I ever saw.
>
> — *Davy Crockett*

With 261,797 square miles (678,054 sq km), Texas occupies about 7 percent of the total land area of the United States. It is 801 miles (1,289 km) from the northwest corner to the southern tip of the state and 773 miles (1,244 km) from the western edge to the eastern boundary of the state.

The natural history of the area includes mountains rising and falling, the creation and evaporation of large inland oceans, volcanic eruptions, and earthquakes. All these factors created the varied landscape of Texas, which includes hills and pine trees, prairies and cacti.

Stretching inland from the Gulf Coast are the Coastal Plains — flat, low prairies filling about two-fifths of the state. Farther north, the Coastal Plains merge into the Great Plains in the Hill Country. Northern Texas, known as the Panhandle because it sticks out from the rest of the state like a handle on a frying pan, is part of the flat, dry High Plains. West of the Pecos River, the Trans-Pecos Region holds the state's most rugged terrain and its highest peak, Guadalupe.

## Highest Point

**Guadalupe Mountains**
Guadalupe Peak
8,749 feet (2,667 m)

## DID YOU KNOW?

**S**outh of Amarillo is the Palo Duro Canyon. Some of the cliffs surrounding the canyon are 1,000 feet (305 m) high.

▼ *From left to right:* A beach in Galveston; wildflowers near Austin; the Texas hill country near Fredericksburg; cowboys injecting yearling cattle with antibiotics; sage brush; Monahan's Sandhills State Park.

## Panhandle Plains

Tributaries of the Red River and the Canadian River run through the High Plains of North Texas. Many trees grow in the river valleys, including cottonwood, mesquite, juniper, hackberry, and elm. On the plains themselves are many types of grasses that protect the surface of the land from erosion. They once served as food for enormous herds of wild buffalo; today they feed herds of cattle.

## Prairies

The Oak Woods and Prairies region was named the Cross-Timbers by early settlers, who found belts of oak forest crossing strips of prairie grassland plunging toward the center of Texas from the northeast corner of the state. Annual rainfall there averages 28 to 40 inches (71 to 102 centimeters) per year. The landscape is one of gently rolling hills. The primary prairie industry is cattle ranching.

## Pinewoods

Rolling terrain covered with pines and oaks and rich bottomlands with tall hardwoods characterize the forests of the eastern Texas Pinewoods. This region is part of a much larger area of pine-hardwood forest that extends into Louisiana, Arkansas, and Oklahoma.

## Coastal Plain

The Texas coast is nearly flat, carved by streams and rivers flowing into the Gulf of Mexico. The region includes barrier islands, salt grass marshes, tallgrass prairies, and oak parklands scattered along the coast.

Just inland from the Gulf Coast are salt marshes, home to many species of birds. Endangered whooping cranes spend their winters at the Aransas National Wildlife Refuge.

**Average January temperature range**
Dallas: 34° to 54°F (1.1° to 12°C)
Houston: 40° to 61°F (4.4° to 16°C)

**Average July temperature range**
Dallas: 75° to 96°F (24° to 35°C)
Houston: 72° to 93°F (22.2° to 34°C)

**Average yearly rainfall**
Dallas: 29.5 inches (75 cm)
Houston: 46 inches (117 cm)

**Average yearly snowfall**
Dallas: 3 to 6 inches (7.6 to 15.2 cm)
Houston: 0 in. (0 cm)

## Major Rivers

**Rio Grande**
1,900 miles (3,060 km)

**Red River**
1,290 miles (2,076 km)

**Brazos River**
1,280 miles (2,060 km)

**Colorado River**
862 miles (1,387 km)

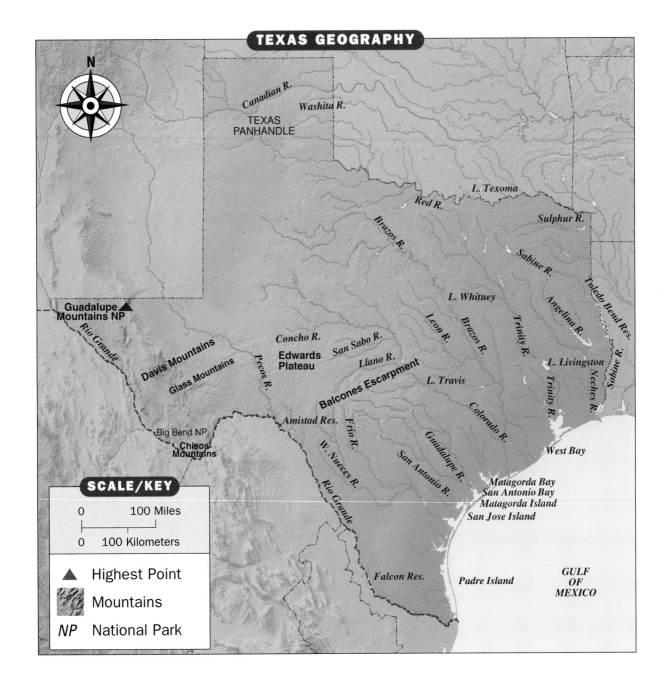

Most of southern Texas consists of coastal plain, dotted with cacti, short grasses, and mesquite trees. Many cattle ranches thrive there, including the King Ranch, which is larger than the state of Rhode Island. Rattlesnakes, coyotes, and horned lizards live in this part of Texas.

Deep in southern Texas is the semitropical Rio Grande Valley. The climate is ideal for farming tropical fruits such as oranges and grapefruits and many varieties of vegetables.

## South Texas Brush Country

This area is characterized by plains of thorny brush vegetation such as mesquite, acacia, and prickly pear, with subtropical woodlands in the Rio Grande Valley.

## Hill Country

Hill Country is the popular name for the Edwards Plateau region of Texas, a landscape with many springs, hills, and steep canyons. The region is home to rare plants and animals and the largest sheep and goat farms in the United States.

The region is characterized by unique minerals and large granite domes such as Enchanted Rock near Fredericksburg.

## Trans-Pecos Region

Most of this area was once covered by vast seas; later, volcanoes and pressures within Earth created mountain ranges. The Guadalupe Mountains include Guadalupe Peak, the highest mountain in Texas at 8,749 feet (2,667 m) above sea level. The Rio Grande, which runs through the Trans-Pecos region, is the world's twentieth largest river and the fifth largest in North America. Wildlife there includes wood rats, snakes, deer, and mountain lions.

## Climate

In summer temperatures in southern Texas can reach well over 110° Fahrenheit (43° Celcius). During winter the northwest averages temperatures in the mid-30s° Fahrenheit (1.5°–2°C).

## Lakes and Rivers

Most of the water in Texas is found underground in enormous reservoirs called aquifers. Rain seeps through the ground to fill the aquifers.

The only large natural lake in Texas is Caddo Lake, located in eastern Texas. Texas also has many lakes and reservoirs that were created when rivers were dammed. These lakes are often used for recreation.

Texas's most famous river is the Rio Grande; others include the Red, Colorado, and Pecos Rivers.

### Wildlife

**B**ecause Texas ranges from lush green tropics to High Plains desert, from sea level at the Gulf Coast to more than 8,000 feet (2,450 m) in the West Texas Mountains, the state is home to a rich variety of wildlife. Texas's diverse environment supports almost 150 different mammals, including armadillos (the official Small Mammal of the State of Texas), 26 species of dolphins and whales, 32 species of bats, plus wolves, bears, ferrets, and 6 species of big cats.

### Major Lakes

**Lake Travis**
60 miles (97 km) long; widest point 4.5 miles (7.2 km)

**Lake Livingston**
52 miles (84 km) long; maximum depth of 90 feet (27 m)

# Black Gold and Beef Cattle

> In one way an oil boom is a mighty
> bad thing, because it gets into your blood and
> almost becomes an obsession.
> Booms are filled with excitement,
> adventure, and drama, but sometimes
> the exit from the scene must be made between
> suns on a pair of mighty weary feet.
>
> — *Sue Sanders,* Our Common Herd, *1940*

Texas has an abundance of rich and varied natural resources. Early in the development of the state's economy, its predominant source of revenue was the export of raw materials and livestock.

Texas' two major industries have historically been oil and cattle ranching, and both are still a prominent part of the state's economic landscape. Texas farms produce a third of the nation's cotton, more than any other state. The state also produces or processes the most asphalt, natural gas, livestock products, chemicals, and refined petroleum products. If Texas were an independent country today, it would have the twelfth largest economy in the world.

## Black Gold

Spanish explorers were the first to find oil in Texas. Forced ashore in July 1542, the men landed in the area between Sabine Pass and High Island and observed oil floating on the surface of the water. They collected it and used it to caulk their vessels.

One of the most popular areas for oil exploration in the upper Gulf Coast area was near Beaumont, where drilling began in 1892. Following several failures, the Gladys City Oil, Gas, and Manufacturing Company hit a gusher on January 10, 1901. In 1901 Spindletop, as the oilfield was christened, produced an estimated 75,000 barrels of oil a day, starting the first oil boom in Texas. The well reached a

### Top Employers
(in order of number of workers employed; totals add up to more than 100% as some residents may hold two or more jobs)

| | |
|---|---|
| Service industries (dry cleaners, restaurants, etc.) | 32.5% |
| Wholesale and retail trade | 22.3% |
| Government | 15.1% |
| Manufacturing | 14.5% |
| Transportation and public utilities | 7.6% |
| Finance, insurance, and real estate | 6.8% |
| Construction | 6.7% |
| Agriculture, forestry, and fisheries | 2.7% |
| Mining | 2.1% |

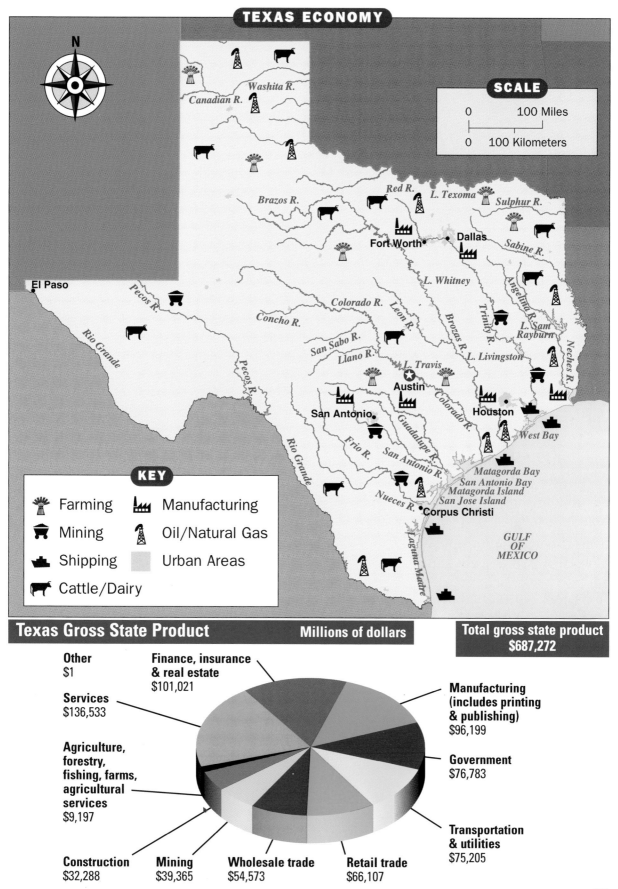

# TEXAS ECONOMY

N

## SCALE
| 0 | 100 Miles |
| 0 | 100 Kilometers |

Canadian R.
Washita R.
Brazos R.
Red R.
L. Texoma
Sulphur R.
Fort Worth
Dallas
Sabine R.
L. Whitney
Colorado R.
Leon R.
Brazos R.
Trinity R.
Angelina R.
L. Sam Rayburn
El Paso
Pecos R.
Concho R.
San Sabo R.
Llano R.
L. Travis
L. Livingston
Neches R.
Rio Grande
Austin
Colorado R.
Houston
Pecos R.
San Antonio
Guadalupe R.
West Bay
Frio R.
San Antonio R.
Matagorda Bay
San Antonio Bay
Matagorda Island
San Jose Island
Nueces R.
Corpus Christi
Rio Grande
Laguna Madre
GULF OF MEXICO

## KEY
- Farming
- Mining
- Shipping
- Cattle/Dairy
- Manufacturing
- Oil/Natural Gas
- Urban Areas

## Texas Gross State Product
**Millions of dollars**

**Total gross state product $687,272**

- Other $1
- Finance, insurance & real estate $101,021
- Services $136,533
- Agriculture, forestry, fishing, farms, agricultural services $9,197
- Construction $32,288
- Mining $39,365
- Wholesale trade $54,573
- Retail trade $66,107
- Transportation & utilities $75,205
- Government $76,783
- Manufacturing (includes printing & publishing) $96,199

production level 17,500,000 barrels in 1902, after which it began to dry up. By 1920 the state census reported oil drilling and refining to be Texas's leading industry.

In 1981 the petroleum industry accounted for more than one-quarter of the state's economy. By 1991 it had fallen to half that level. The proportion of state government revenue from the petroleum industry declined to 7 percent in 1993, down from 28 percent ten years earlier.

## A Breed Apart

By the end of the Texas Revolution, cattle ranching had become a dominant industry. Longhorns, a hybrid of Spanish and English cattle, roamed wild on the plains. Texas ranchers crossbred them with domesticated cattle to create a breed that was durable enough for the extremes of the state's geography and weather, yet yielded more meat per animal. From 1867 to 1887, more than six million cattle were moved from Texas ranches to slaughterhouses in the Midwest.

In the 1990s livestock accounted for more than half of the state's agricultural cash receipts. Cattle provides 70 percent of the state's cash receipts in livestock. Texas was first nationally in dairy and beef cattle, sheep, lambs, and goats.

**Made in Texas**

**Leading farm products and crops**
- Cattle and calves
- Corn
- Cotton
- Hay
- Wheat
- Sorghum
- Potatoes
- Grapefruit
- Chicken
- Milk, cream, and other dairy products

**Other products**
- Chemicals
- Petroleum, gas, and coal
- Computers and electronics
- Fabricated metal
- Transportation equipment

| International Airports | | |
|---|---|---|
| **Airport** | **Location** | **Passengers per year (approx)** |
| Dallas/Fort Worth International | Dallas/Fort Worth | 60,687,122 |
| George Bush Intercontinental | Houston | 35,246,176 |
| San Antonio International | San Antonio | 7,307,282 |
| El Paso International | El Paso | 2,381,731 |

## Timber!

Early settlers found 150-foot (46-m) pine trees in East Texas, with trunks so wide that three men together could not link hands around them. The generation after World War II saw a revolution in the Texas lumber industry. The introduction of modern logging and milling equipment made it possible for the production of a wider variety of wood products.

The East Texas landscape is still mostly forested, and many areas are managed by the timber industry. Several sites have old-growth stands that suggest how the primitive forests might have looked. The forests in East Texas extend over forty-three counties and provide almost all of the state's timber.

At the turn of the twentieth century, the timber industry was the state's largest manufacturing enterprise, first in generating income and the largest employer in Texas. By 1982 lumber and forest products still ranked among the top ten products manufactured in the state.

▼ Three of Texas's twentieth-century pioneers — Apollo 11 astronauts and lunar explorers Neil Armstrong, Mike Collins, and Edwin "Buzz" Aldrin.

## More Than a Lone Star

Before World War II manufacturing in Texas centered on processing raw materials, notably petroleum and agricultural products. Since then Texas has experienced significant industrial expansion, especially in high-tech industries. The future growth of manufacturing in Texas will be tied to new industries that have sprung up with advances in science and technology. The Lyndon B. Johnson Space Center in Houston has led to the growth of industries related to space exploration. Cities all over Texas have benefited from the work provided by the space center.

# A Step Ahead

> It is an axiom in political science that unless a people are educated and enlightened it is idle to expect the continuance of civil liberty or the capacity for self-government.
>
> *Texas Declaration of Independence, March 2, 1836*

**T**exas is governed from the city of Austin. Like the government of the United States, Texas's government is divided into three branches: legislative, executive, and judicial.

The job of the Texas Legislature, called the "Lege" by many Texans, is to make laws for the people of Texas. The Lege is *bicameral*, or has two houses. Its houses are the Senate and the House of Representatives. Currently there are 31 Texas state senators and 150 members of the House of Representatives; they meet in sessions of 140 days starting on the second Tuesday in January every other year in odd-numbered years.

## The Executive Branch

The executive branch is headed by the governor, who is elected for a four-year term. The governor is responsible for creating a budget for the state, making sure the laws are carried out, and running the state's day-to-day affairs.

## The Legislative Branch

The Texas Legislature operates very much like the United States Congress. Legislators can introduce proposals for new laws, called bills. Each bill is discussed by the representatives and then put to a vote. If more than half of the

> **DID YOU KNOW?**
>
> **W**hen Texas became a state, it reserved the right to divide itself into five new states. This could still be done if wished.

| The Legislature | | | |
|---|---|---|---|
| **House** | **Number of Members** | **Length of Term** | **Term Limits** |
| Senate | 31 senators | 4 years | None |
| House of Representatives | 150 representatives | 2 years | None |

representatives vote yes, then the bill passes and moves on to the senate, where it is also discussed and voted on. If the bill passes in the senate, it is sent to the governor, who decides whether or not to sign it into law.

If the governor vetoes, or refuses to sign, a bill but the members of the legislature want the bill to become law anyway, the legislature can hold another vote. If two-thirds of the members of each house vote yes, then the bill becomes law despite the governor's veto.

| Elected Posts in the Executive Branch | | |
|---|---|---|
| Office | Length of Term | Term Limits |
| Governor | 4 years | 2 terms |
| Lieutenant Governor | 4 years | 2 terms |
| Secretary of State | 4 years | 2 terms |
| Attorney General | 4 years | 2 terms |
| Comptroller of Public Accounts | 4 years | 2 terms |

## The Judicial Branch

The judicial branch enforces the laws of Texas. The state's highest court, the nine-member Texas Supreme Court, rules on many cases each year. Within each county and city are district courts to try local cases. The Texas Court of Criminal Appeals is where convicted criminals can turn to ask for a new trial if they believe they are innocent or were wrongly convicted.

**DID YOU KNOW?**

■In 1960 Texas politician Lyndon Baines Johnson was elected vice president of the United States, to serve under President John F. Kennedy. On November 22, 1963, President Kennedy was assassinated while riding in a motorcade through downtown Dallas, Texas. Lyndon Johnson, known as LBJ, was sworn in as president aboard the presidential airplane that same day.

**DID YOU KNOW?**

■In Texas the lieutenant governor is elected separately from the governor, and each can be a member of a different party.

◄ The Texas state capitol building was built between 1885 and 1888.

## State Politicians

Texas history is filled with interesting politicians, from Sam Houston, one of the state's first U.S. senators, to Barbara Jordan, the first African-American woman elected to the Texas senate. In recent years Texas has been shaped by leaders such as former governor Ann Richards. Texas politicians have gone on to national roles, too. President Dwight Eisenhower was a Texan, as was President Lyndon Baines Johnson (known as LBJ); George Herbert Walker Bush moved to Texas after World War II, making him an honorary Texan by the time he was elected U.S. president in 1988. His son George W. Bush was narrowly elected president of the United States in 2000. Justice Sandra Day O'Connor, born in El Paso, was the first woman appointed to the United States Supreme Court.

At times in its history, Texas has been politically progressive. In 1919 it was the first Southern state to ratify the Nineteenth Amendment, which granted women the right to vote. Texas had already granted women the right to vote in state party primaries the previous year. Texas Federal District Judge Sarah Hughes is the only woman ever to have administered the oath of office to a U.S. president (LBJ, following the assassination of John F. Kennedy in 1963). When Governor William Clements was elected in 1978, he became the first Republican governor to serve in Texas since the post-Civil War Reconstruction period.

Texas today tends to be politically mixed. Unlike many other states, voters in Texas do not register a party affiliation and can vote in either the Democratic or Republican primary elections.

**Four Texans have served as president of the United States**

## DWIGHT DAVID EISENHOWER

(1953–1961) The thirty-fourth president of the United States was born in Texas but raised in Kansas. As General Eisenhower, he was the supreme commander of the U.S. and Allied troops in Europe during World War II and then of the North Atlantic Treaty Organization (NATO) troops in Europe after the war. In 1952 the Republican Party convinced him to run for president. He was elected and served two terms. During his administration Eisenhower concentrated on world peace and the domestic front, desegregated the Armed Forces, and upheld the mandate to desegregate public schools by sending troops to Arkansas to enforce the Supreme Court's decision.

## LYNDON BAINES JOHNSON

(1963–1969) Born near Stonewall in 1908, Lyndon Johnson (known as LBJ) was elected to the U.S. House of Representatives and U.S. Senate. After President John F. Kennedy was assassinated in 1963, then Vice President LBJ became the thirty-sixth president. During his presidency he passed many civil rights programs, including the Civil Rights Act of 1964. He was elected president by a landslide in November 1964. LBJ devoted himself to carrying out the legacy of John F. Kennedy. He also championed the National Aeronautics and Space Administration. Johnson was very popular in the years immediately following his assuming the presidency but lost popularity because of his support for the Vietnam War. He withdrew his candidacy for reelection in 1968 and retired from public life.

## GEORGE HERBERT WALKER BUSH

(1989–1993) Although George Bush was born in Massachusetts, he moved to Texas as a young man to work in the oil industry. In 1966 he ran for and was elected to the U.S. House of Representatives. He served two terms. He gave up his seat in 1970 in an unsuccessful bid for a seat in the Senate but was then appointed ambassador to the United Nations (UN). Thereafter he was appointed to a variety of public offices. He served two terms under Ronald Reagan as vice president and was then elected the forty-first president. He served one term, during which time he sent U.S. troops into Panama and initiated Operation Desert Storm in a successful bid to drive Iraq out of neighboring Kuwait.

## GEORGE WALKER BUSH

(2001–) Although born in Connecticut, George W. Bush grew up largely in Midland and Houston, Texas. He is the son of the forty-first president, George Bush. In 1994 George W. Bush was elected governor of Texas, and he was reelected in 1998. In 1999 Bush announced his candidacy for the presidency, and the following year he narrowly defeated Vice President Al Gore by winning the majority of the electoral college votes, although losing the popular vote. The forty-third U.S. president found his new administration challenged by the terrorist attacks on New York City and the Pentagon in Virginia during his first year in office.

# Texas Two-Step

> This soil has nourished me as the banks of the lovely Guadalupe River nourish cypress trees, as the Brazos bottoms nourish the wild peach, as the gentle slopes of East Texas nourish the sweet-smelling pines, as the barren, rocky ridges along the Pecos nourish the daggered lechuguilla. I am at home here, and I want not only to know about my home land, I want to live intelligently on it.
>
> — *J. Frank Dobie,*
> **Guide to Life and Literature of the Southwest**

E ven grander than the sheer size of Texas is its cultural diversity. People from all over the world have come, weaving a vibrant tapestry of languages, traditions, and art forms. An introduction to that tapestry can be found at The Institute of Texan Cultures in San Antonio, which highlights twenty-six of the cultural and ethnic groups that make the Lone Star State what it is.

## Food

Another way to appreciate the cultural history of Texas is through its food. No other state has as many cook-offs, fry-offs, festivals, jamborees, and other celebrations of food — Turkey Trots, Watermelon Thumps, Chili Cookoffs, and even a Jalapeño Eating Contest!

Several types of cuisine are characteristic of Texas. As its name suggests, *Tex-Mex* is a Texas version of traditional Mexican cuisine. It is

rich with Mexican flavors and ingredients but prepared in U.S. southern style. You will not find many Tex-Mex dishes in Mexico. Or if you do, they will look very different. The official state dish — chili — has almost as many different recipes as there are Texans. No one is sure of its exact origins, but it became popular around 1850 when the "chili queens" of San Antonio stirred up huge vats of the stew to sell at the military plaza. The world was first introduced to chili at the 1893 Chicago World's Fair in a booth simply called "San Antonio Chili." The International Championship Chili Cook-Off is a Texas tradition held every year in the town of Terlingua. Texas also claims to have invented the barbecue — in the back rooms of Central Texas meat markets early in the nineteenth century.

## Music

One of the Lone Star State's most distinctive musical forms is *Tejano*. In a way, it is the musical counterpart of Tex-Mex cuisine. Tejano's blend of Mexican and American vocals, instruments, and styles is a perfect fit for the state's blended heritage and culture.

Texas is home to a wide range of music, art, and theater. Every major city has a symphony orchestra, and Texans also enjoy the music of thousands of country-and-western

### Texas Blues

The Texas blues are characterized by high-voiced singing accompanied by guitar lines picked out on single strings rather than strummed chords. Blind Lemon Jefferson (1897–1929) was by far the most influential Texas bluesman. Blind from birth, he became a wandering musician in his teens, creating the distinctive Texas blues sound from the sounds he heard along the way. Texas blues was later given a rock dimension by musicians like Stevie Ray Vaughan and ZZ Top.

bands. Almost every Texan knows how to dance the Texas Two-Step and the Cotton-Eyed Joe. Two of Texas's most famous country musicians are Willie Nelson and George Strait.

## Colleges and Universities

The two best-known universities in Texas are the University of Texas at Austin (UT Austin) and Texas A&M University in College Station.

A&M, the state's first public institution of higher education, was opened in 1876 as the Agricultural and Mechanical College of Texas. In 1963 the name of the institution was changed to Texas A&M University.

UT Austin is the largest school in the University of Texas system, which includes fifteen universities around the state. UT and A&M are archrivals in sporting events.

Texas is also home to the University of Houston system, Trinity University and the University of the Incarnate Word in San Antonio, the University of North Texas in Denton, and many other two- and four-year colleges.

### Texas A&M University Fires Up Football Season

**A&M** is known for its tradition of building an enormous bonfire each year before competing with UT. The tradition began in 1919. In the 1960s the bonfire became a multi-tiered structure; in 2000 the bonfire collapsed while under construction, killing nine people and injuring many others. As a result, the university took a two-year hiatus from the bonfire in order to institute new safety procedures.

◀ A football game at the University of Texas at Austin.

## State and National Parks

Texas has four national forests (Angelina, Davy Crockett, Sabine, and Sam Houston), two national parks (Big Bend and Guadalupe Mountains), one national seashore (Padre Island), one national preserve (the Big Thicket), two national recreation areas (Amistad and Lake Meredith) and one national monument (Alibates Flint Quarries). There are also more than 120 state parks, state historical parks, and state historical sites in Texas.

Caddoan Mounds Historic Park is located in Alto, Texas. The area was home to mound-building people of Caddoan origin who lived in the region for between five hundred and one thousand years, beginning around 800 A.D. These prehistoric people had a heritage rooted in older woodland cultures of the Mississippi Valley and dominated the East Texas forests until the early days of European exploration.

Dinosaur Valley State Park is a scenic area set astride the Paluxy River. It is best known for its dinosaur tracks, which are some of the best preserved in the world. In addition to white-tailed deer, coyote, bobcat, raccoon, beaver, skunk, opossum, armadillo, fox squirrel, and rabbit, visitors may spot Texas longhorns, many of which still range free in the park.

Galveston Island State Park is located in the city of Galveston on the Gulf Coast. This is where Spanish explorer Cabeza de Vaca and his crew were shipwrecked. The great hurricane of 1900 devastated the island, killing more than five thousand people.

## Sports

Texas is home to several major sports teams. The Dallas Cowboys play in the National Football League. After winning the Super Bowl in 1992 and 1993, the Cowboys became one of only three NFL teams to claim four world championships. Another professional football team — the Houston Texans — joins the NFL as of the 2002 season.

Texas is also home to a serious basketball rivalry among its National Basketball Association teams — the San Antonio Spurs, the Houston Rockets, and the Dallas Mavericks. The Rockets won the NBA championship in 1993–1994, and the Spurs won in 1998–1999. Houston also fields a WNBA team, the Comets, winners of four straight WBNA championships from 1997-2000.

No stranger to "America's game," Texas also boasts two baseball teams — the Houston Astros and Texas Rangers. In 1965 the Astrodome — the world's first air-conditioned sports arena — opened. The Rangers came to Texas in 1972 and were one of the teams on which pitching great Nolan Ryan starred.

Although snow and ice are rare in most of Texas, the

**DID YOU KNOW?**

**N**inepins was the most popular form of bowling in much of the United States from colonial times until the early nineteenth century, when it was outlawed in many areas and replaced by tenpins. Today ninepin bowling has disappeared from all of the United States except Texas.

| Sport | Team | Home |
| --- | --- | --- |
| Baseball | Houston Astros | Enron Field, Houston |
| | Texas Rangers | The Ball Park, Arlington |
| Basketball | Houston Rockets | Compaq Center Arena, Houston |
| | San Antonio Spurs | Alamo Dome Arena, San Antonio |
| | Dallas Mavericks | American Airlines Center, Dallas |
| Women's Basketball | Houston Comets | Compaq Center Arena, Houston |
| Football | Dallas Cowboys | Texas Stadium, Irving |
| | Houston Texans | Reliant Stadium, Houston |
| Hockey | Dallas Stars | American Airlines Center, Dallas |
| Soccer | Dallas Burn | Cotton Bowl, Dallas |

state is also home to an ice hockey team, the Dallas Stars. The Stars' team name refers to a famous verse from the song "Deep in the Heart of Texas":

*The stars at night*
*Are big and bright*
*[clap clap clap clap]*
*Deep in the heart of Texas!*

▼ The American Quarter Horse Museum in Amarillo is dedicated to preserving the history and heritage of this U.S. breed that was vitally important to the success of the cattle industry. The name *quarter horse* comes from the fact that they must be one-fourth thoroughbred to deserve the name.

# Giants of Texas

There is a growing feeling that perhaps Texas is really another country, a place where the skies, the disasters, the diamonds, the politicians, the women, the fortunes, [and] the football players . . . are all bigger than anywhere else.

— *The* Boston Globe, *August 1966*

Following are only a few of the thousands of people who were born, died, or spent most of their lives in Texas and made extraordinary contributions to the state and the nation.

## SAM HOUSTON
**POLITICAL LEADER**

**BORN:** *March 2, 1793, Rockbridge County, VA*
**DIED:** *July 26, 1863, Huntsville*

In his youth Sam Houston ran away from home in Tennessee to live with the Cherokee. He became the Cherokee's spokesperson in Washington, D.C. In 1832 President Andrew Jackson sent Houston to the Mexican province of Texas to negotiate treaties with Native Americans there. Houston led a band of U.S. settlers who overthrew Mexican rule in 1836. Texas was an independent republic for nine years with Houston as its president (1836 to 1838 and 1841 to 1844). He helped negotiate Texas's statehood in 1845 and served as senator until 1859. In 1859 he was elected governor of Texas. When he refused to sign an oath of loyalty to the Confederacy in the Civil War, he was turned out of public office.

## STEPHEN AUSTIN
**POLITICAL LEADER**

**BORN:** *November 3, 1793, Austinville, VA*
**DIED:** *December 27, 1836, Austin*

In 1819 Austin's father purchased a tract of 200,000 acres (80,935 hectares) in Texas from the Mexican government and received permission to settle three hundred families from the United States in the territory. When Austin's father died in 1821 without having fulfilled this plan, he took it up. Austin established a settlement on the Brazos River in 1822. The Mexican government gave Austin the authority to represent the colonists. In this role he served the interests of his slave-holding settlers by preventing a ban on slavery in the colony. Austin consistently favored remaining under Mexican rule, although many in the settlement wanted Texas to become independent or to join the United States. Eventually Austin took up this cause but died before Texas became a state.

# HENRY OSSIAN FLIPPER

## SOLDIER AND ENGINEER

**BORN:** *March 21, 1856, Thomasville, GA*
**DIED:** *May 3, 1940, Atlanta, GA*

**B**orn into slavery, Flipper became the first African-American graduate of the U.S. Military Academy. As an officer in the Tenth Cavalry, he was stationed at several forts in Texas and was one of the "Buffalo Soldiers" of the day. While at Fort Sill, he created "Flipper's Ditch," now a national landmark, when he supervised the drainage of ponds containing malaria-carrying mosquitoes. West Point annually gives out an award in his name to the graduate who best exemplifies "the highest qualities of leadership, self-discipline, and perseverance in the face of unusual difficulties" while a cadet.

# SCOTT JOPLIN

## MUSICIAN AND COMPOSER

**BORN:** *November 24, 1868, Texarkana*
**DIED:** *April 1, 1917, New York, NY*

**S**cott Joplin was born in 1868 in Texarkana, the son of a freed slave. He became famous for popularizing a form of music called rag or ragtime. He wrote over five hundred pieces of music, including two operas and a ballet. Today he is best known for his rags, especially "The Entertainer," which was used as the theme to the Oscar-winning movie *The Sting* in 1973. That made rag music popular in a whole new way. Joplin died in 1917 and was never famous during his lifetime, but he was awarded a posthumous Pulitzer Prize in 1976 for his contributions to American music.

# DR. MICHAEL DeBAKEY

## SURGEON

**BORN:** *September 7, 1908, Lake Charles, LA*

**M**ichael DeBakey is considered one of the world's greatest heart surgeons. In 1948 he became professor of surgery and chairman of the department of surgery at Baylor College of Medicine in Houston. In 1954 Dr. DeBakey made medical history by performing heart surgery on public television. He became a leader in the field of cardiovascular medicine, and in 1964 he performed the nation's first coronary bypass operation.

# BABE DIDRIKSON

## ATHLETE

**BORN:** *June 26, 1914, Port Arthur*
**DIED:** *September 27, 1956, Galveston*

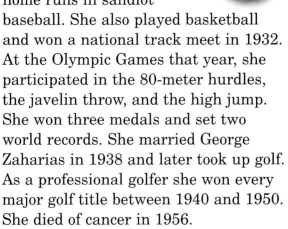

**B**orn in 1914, Mildred Ella Didrikson got the nickname "Babe" (after Babe Ruth) while hitting home runs in sandlot baseball. She also played basketball and won a national track meet in 1932. At the Olympic Games that year, she participated in the 80-meter hurdles, the javelin throw, and the high jump. She won three medals and set two world records. She married George Zaharias in 1938 and later took up golf. As a professional golfer she won every major golf title between 1940 and 1950. She died of cancer in 1956.

# HENRY B. GONZALEZ
## POLITICAL LEADER
**BORN:** *May 3, 1916, San Antonio*
**DIED:** *November 29, 2000, San Antonio*

**H**enry Gonzalez, a native of San Antonio, in 1956 became the first Mexican American elected to the state senate since 1846. In 1961 he became the first Mexican American elected from Texas to serve in the U.S. House of Representatives. In 1994, while serving his thirty-third year in Congress, Gonzalez accepted the Profile in Courage award. He is the only Texan ever to win it. He died in 2000.

# SANDRA DAY O'CONNOR
## SUPREME COURT JUSTICE
**BORN:** *March 26, 1930, El Paso*

**B**orn in El Paso in 1930, Sandra Day O'Connor was the first woman to serve on the United States Supreme Court. She is known as a moderate conservative. O'Connor grew up on a family ranch in Arizona and graduated from Stanford University in 1950 and Stanford Law School in 1952. She worked as a lawyer, an assistant attorney general, and a state senator in Arizona. In July 1981 President Ronald Reagan chose her as his first appointee to the U.S. Supreme Court, and, after her confirmation by the Senate, she was sworn in as an associate justice on September 25, 1981.

# ALVIN AILEY, JR.
## DANCER AND CHOREOGRAPHER
**BORN:** *January 5, 1931, Rogers*
**DIED:** *December 1, 1989, New York, NY*

**I**n 1942 Alvin Ailey moved with his family from Texas to Los Angeles, where he became a member of the Lester Horton Dance Theater. He moved to New York City in 1954 and began an acting career, while also studying dance with many of the greats of modern dance, including Martha Graham. In 1958 Ailey formed his own dance company, The Alvin Ailey American Dance Theater. Composed primarily of African Americans, the company toured the world, performing works by Ailey and other choreographers. Their signature piece was an early work by Ailey called "Revelations" (1960), which is danced to the music of black spirituals. The company he established has continued to perform since his death. An estimated nineteen million people in forty-eight states and sixty-eight countries have enjoyed the productions.

▼ Alvin Ailey's "Revelations."

## WILLIE NELSON
**MUSICIAN**

**BORN:** *April 30, 1933, Abbott*

**B**orn in 1933 in Abbott, Willie Nelson learned to play guitar from his grandfather. He was playing music at local dances by the time he was ten. As a young man he served in the Air Force; then he became a disc jockey. Nelson began his songwriting career in Nashville, Tennessee. He returned to Texas in 1972 after having won a spot in the Songwriters Hall of Fame. During the 1980s he organized annual Farm Aid concerts to raise money for farmers. In addition to the many hits he has recorded on his own, he has also recorded with at least seventy-five other singers. In 1990 the Internal Revenue Service claimed that he owed $16.7 million in unpaid taxes and seized his assets. Nelson is still one of Texas's most popular musicians.

## BARBARA JORDAN
**POLITICAL LEADER**

**BORN:** *February 21, 1936, Houston*
**DIED:** *January 17, 1996, Austin*

**B**orn in Houston in 1936, Barbara Jordan began her political career in 1966 when she became the first African-American woman elected to the Texas senate. In 1972 she became a U.S. representative and won national recognition serving on the Judiciary Committee during the investigation of the Watergate scandal. In 1994 she was awarded the Medal of Freedom, the nation's highest civilian honor. She died in 1996.

## BUDDY HOLLY
**MUSICIAN**

**BORN:** *September 7, 1936, Lubbock*
**DIED:** *February 3, 1959, near Mason City, IA*

**C**harles Hardin, known as Buddy Holly, was a songwriter and an early rock-and-roll musician. Holly and his band, the Crickets, were among the first white rock-and-roll bands to play their own songs. Holly wrote most of their hits, including "Peggy Sue," "That'll Be the Day," and "Maybe Baby." He died in a plane crash in 1959, at the age of twenty-two.

## SANDRA CISNEROS
**WRITER**

**BORN:** *December 20, 1954, Chicago, IL*

**S**andra Cisneros moved to San Antonio in the early 1980s. She is widely considered to be one of the stars of today's literary world. Her poems, stories, and essays draw on her Latina heritage. Cisneros's books include *Woman Hollering Creek and Other Stories, The House on Mango Street,* and *Hairs / Pelitos,* a story for children. She has won many prestigious literary awards, a MacArthur fellowship, and a National Endowment for the Arts fellowship.

# Texas

## History At-A-Glance

**1519**
The Spanish explorer Alonso Alvarez de Pineda maps the Texas coast. Spain claims the land.

**1528**
Spanish explorers Pánfilo de Narváez and Álvar Nuñez Jérez de la Frontera-Cabeza de Vaca are shipwrecked near what is now Galveston; the survivors make their way to Mexico City with tales of the fabled "Seven Cities of Gold."

**1682**
The Spanish establish Corpus Christi de la Isleta near what is now El Paso; it is the first Spanish mission and pueblo in Texas.

**1685**
French explorer Robert Cavelier, sieur de La Salle, establishes Fort St. Louis in the Matagorda Bay area, marking the beginning of French exploration in Texas.

**1821**
Mexico becomes independent from Spain. Stephen F. Austin receives permission from Mexico to create an Anglo settlement with three hundred families.

**1835**
The Texas Revolution begins with the Battle of Gonzales.

**1836**
The Battle of the Alamo is won by Mexican forces under General Santa Anna; Texas declares independence from Mexico. The Battle of San Jacinto is won by the Texans, and Texas becomes an independent Republic.

**1845**
Texas becomes part of the United States.

---

**1600**          **1700**

---

**1492**
Christopher Columbus comes to the New World.

**1607**
Capt. John Smith and three ships land on Virginia coast and start first English settlement in New World — Jamestown.

**1754–63**
French and Indian War.

**1773**
Boston Tea Party.

**1776**
Declaration of Independence adopted July 4.

**1777**
Articles of Confederation adopted by Continental Congress.

**1787**
U.S. Constitution written.

**1812–14**
War of 1812.

# United States

## History At-A-Glance

**1900**
A hurricane destroys most of Galveston and leaves over five thousand dead.

**1901**
Oil is discovered at Spindletop Hill near Beaumont.

**1950**
Herman Marion Sweatt becomes the first African American admitted to the University of Texas Law School.

**1963**
President John F. Kennedy is assassinated in Dallas.

**1965**
The Astrodome, the world's first air-conditioned football and baseball stadium, opens in Houston.

**1990**
Ann Richards is the second woman to be elected governor of Texas.

**1993**
After fifty-one days a fiery disaster marks the end of the standoff between federal law-enforcement officers and Branch Davidians at the cult's compound in Waco.

**2000**
Texas Governor George W. Bush is elected president of the United States.

**1800**       **1900**       **2000**

**1848**
Gold is discovered in California and draws 80,000 prospectors in the 1849 gold rush.

**1861–65**
Civil War.

**1869**
Transcontinental railroad is completed.

**1917–18**
U.S. involvement in World War I.

**1929**
Stock market crash ushers in Great Depression.

**1941–45**
U.S. involvement in World War II.

**1950–53**
United States fights in the Korean War.

**1964–73**
U.S. involvement in Vietnam War.

**2000**
George W. Bush wins the closest presidential election in history.

**2001**
A terrorist attack in which four hijacked airliners crash into New York City's World Trade Center, the Pentagon, and farmland in western Pennsylvania leaves thousands dead or injured.

▼ Goose Creek oil field, circa 1919.

# Festivals and Fun For All

Check web site for exact date and directions.

▲ *Austin City Limits,* featuring country music star Lyle Lovett.

## Balloon Liftoff Festival, Houston

The NASA/Johnson Space Center sponsors a festival complete with hot-air balloon competitions, evening balloon glows, skydiving exhibitions, arts and crafts exhibits, entertainment, and aviation equipment displays.
www.ballunarfestival.com

## Bedford Blues Festival & Art Fair, Dallas

Every Labor Day weekend this outdoor blues bash showcases some of the best local, regional, and national blues talent.
www.meifestivals.com/blues.html

## A Celebration of Whooping Cranes and Other Birds, Port Aransas

Wintering migratory birds flock to the Texas wetlands in Port Aransas.
www.portaransas.org/cranes.asp

## Central Texas State Fair, Bell County

Five days of livestock shows, a great carnival, a dunking booth, strolling acts, fabulous foods, and lots more.
www.centraltexasstatefair.com

## The Poteet Strawberry Festival®, Poteet

One of the oldest Texas events, the annual Poteet Strawberry Festival® is also the state's largest agricultural festival.
www.strawberryfestival.com

## Scottish Festival and Highland Games, Arlington

Outstanding entertainment — music, games, and much more.
www.texasscottishfestival.com

## The Seabrook Music Festival, Seabrook

Four music stages, plus a carnival, plays, arts and crafts, and much more.
www.allpointspro.com/html/
seabrookmusicfestival.html

## Texas Book Festival, Austin

A celebration of books and Texas writers.
www.texasbookfestival.org

## Texas Butterfly Festival, Mission

Located in the southernmost tip of the Lower Rio Grande Valley, Mission is the most bio-diverse region in the United States with over 260 species of butterflies. A mecca for butterfly watching year around.
www.texasbutterfly.com

## Texas Film Festival, College Station

Join in the fun at the largest student-run film festival in the nation.
TxFilmFest.tamu.edu

## Texas Jazz Festival, Corpus Christi

For over forty years the Texas Jazz Festival has been recognized by jazz aficionados as one of the best festivals going.
www.texasjazz-fest.org

▶ A game of chess in San Antonio.

### Texas Renaissance Festival, Plantersville

Unique artisans from around the world, plus games and rides, music and drama.

www.texrenfest.com

### Texas Rice Festival, Winnie

Winnie hosts a harvest festival every October, with food, crafts, and games.

www.texasricefestival.org

### State Fair of Texas, Dallas

One of Texas's largest state fairs.

www.bigtex.com

### Texas State Science & Engineering Fair, Austin

Texans demonstrate their love and knowledge of science.

science.uta.edu/EMTSEF/home.asp

▼ The River Walk in San Antonio.

## Books

Burnett, Carolyn Mitchell. *The First Texans*. Austin, TX: Eakin Press, 1995. The history and cultures of Texas's Native American population.

Kahn, Sharon. *Brave Black Women: From Slavery to the Space Shuttle*. Austin, TX: University of Texas Press, 1997. Learn about the remarkable achievements of African-American women in Texas.

Tannery Jones, Martha. *Terror from the Gulf: A Hurricane in Galveston*. Dallas, TX: Hendrick-Long Publishing, 1999. The hurricane that devastated Galveston in 1900.

McComb, David G. *Texas: An Illustrated History*. New York: Oxford University Press, 1992. Texas from ten thousand years ago to the 1990s.

Warren, Betsy. *Moses Austin and Stephen F. Austin: A Gone to Texas Dual Biography*. Austin, TX: Hendrick-Long Publishing, 1996. Read more about the Austins and their role in the settlement and statehood of Texas.

## Web Sites

▶ The official state web site
www.state.tx.us

▶ The official state capital site
www.ci.austin.tx.us/defaultfull.htm

▶ The Texas State Historical Society
www.tsha.utexas.edu

▶ Texas Historical Commission
www.thc.state.tx.us

▶ The Handbook of Texas Online
www.tsha.utexas.edu/handbook/online

## Films

Burns, Ken, and Steven Ives. *New Perspectives on the West*. Washington, D.C.: The West Films, Inc./WETA, 2001. An eight-part series on the U.S. West, the first three episodes being of particular interest in the study of Texas. See the PBS site www.pbs.org/weta/thewest for more information.